I0465084

Table of contents

Introduction

Credit scoring uses statistical modeling to predict whether a consumer will default on his or her debts. The quantitative estimates that these methods produce, called "credit scores," allow lenders to rank order consumers in terms of the credit risk they pose and are used pervasively in all aspects of consumer lending. As a result, having a good credit score is important for credit access. Moreover, since credit scores, or other scores generated from credit report information such as insurance scores, can be used for underwriting other financial services products, including checking accounts and property and casualty insurance, a good credit score and credit report may provide benefits beyond credit access.

While there are many different types of scoring models, those based on credit history information, such as the FICO and VantageScore, are the most widely used. These models generally rely on the credit histories compiled by nationwide credit reporting agencies (NCRAs). These records detail the credit accounts each consumer has held (called "tradelines"), collection agency accounts, monetary-related public records (*e.g.*, tax liens, bankruptcy filings), and records of inquiries made by lenders in connection with a consumer-initiated credit application.

Even among consumers who have credit records – and many do not – NCRA records may contain little credit history information. This will occur when the consumer has little or no recent experience with credit in the United States or predominantly uses "non-traditional" sources of credit (such as payday lenders or pawnshops), which generally do not furnish account information to the NCRAs (although they sometimes furnish information to specialty consumer reporting agencies). With little information available with which to gauge the consumer's riskiness, such "thin file" consumers generally receive lower scores as a result. In some cases, the amount of information is so sparse that model builders will deem the credit record "unscorable" and no score will be generated. Having a thin or unscorable credit record generally reduces access to credit.

Despite their thin or unscorable records, many of these consumers may be creditworthy, meaning that they are likely to repay their debts. However, because of the limited credit history reflected in their credit records, credit scoring models cannot distinguish them from less creditworthy consumers who also have thin credit records. A frequently suggested solution to this problem is to supplement the credit history information of these consumers with additional data. Alternative sources of data, such as rental histories or utility payments, have been shown to increase the credit scores of many creditworthy consumers with thin files (Turner, *et al.*, 2006).

Another potential source of information that could enhance consumers' credit scores is data on remittance transfers, which are certain electronic transfers of funds made by U.S. consumers to recipients abroad. Towards this end, Section 1073(e) of the Dodd-Frank Wall Street Reform and Consumer Protection Act required the Director of the Consumer Financial Protection Bureau (CFPB) to report within one year of the law's enactment regarding, among other issues, the feasibility of and impediments to using remittance information in credit scoring. The Bureau issued that report on July 20, 2011.

In the report, the Bureau noted that there were a number of business and legal issues that stood as potential impediments to incorporating remittance history into credit files, including some relating to whether remittance transfer providers would be willing to act as data furnishers to NCRAs and others relating to whether NCRAs and those who build scoring models would be willing to devote the time and resources required to incorporate this information into credit files and to build credit scoring models using such data. The Bureau noted, however, that it would conduct further empirical analyses to better address the potential for remittance information to enhance consumer credit scores. In this report, we discuss the empirical research completed to date by CFPB staff regarding whether data on remittance transfers can enhance the credit scores of consumers. As discussed in our earlier report (CFPB, 2011), "enhancing the credit scores of consumers" can be interpreted as either raising the credit scores of consumers who send remittance transfers or as improving credit score predictiveness to more accurately reflect credit risk. Our analysis covers both interpretations.

The analysis is conducted in two parts. The first part focuses on consumers who have unscorable credit records and evaluates whether information about remittance histories has the potential to improve the predictiveness of credit scoring models sufficiently to allow scores to be generated for records that are unscorable based on credit history alone. The results of this analysis suggest that remittance histories add very little to the predictiveness of a credit scoring model for these consumers.

The second part of the analysis examines the potential of remittance histories to raise the credit scores of consumers with scorable credit records. This part of the analysis evaluates whether, after controlling for credit scores, remittance history information is negatively associated with subsequent delinquency. If so, remittance histories have predictive value over and above the information currently incorporated in credit scores that would be expected to result in higher credit scores for consumers who send remittance transfers. The results of our analysis suggest that, to the extent they have additional predictive value, remittance histories are positively associated with delinquency. This appears unrelated to the remittance transfers themselves and instead results from selection effects that cannot be adequately explained by the data. Given the positive correlation, building a credit scoring model that includes remittance history information is unlikely to increase the credit scores of consumers who send remittance transfers.

2. Data

To address the issues specified in Section 1073(e), CFPB staff assembled a unique source of data that combined information about remittance transfers with consumer credit record data. To construct this dataset, the CFPB partnered with a large remittance transfer provider (RTP) that selected a random sample of 500,000 anonymous consumers who sent one or more remittance transfers during 2007 and for whom the RTP had contact information (the "remitter sample"). The sampling frame that was used to draw this sample was based on consumers (as opposed to remittance transfers), so that a consumer who sent many transfers had the same probability of being selected as a consumer who sent only one.

Once the remitter sample was selected, the RTP identified all transactions made by those consumers during the period January 1, 2007 to December 31, 2008. For each transaction, the RTP compiled the date and amount of the remittance transfer, the mode of payment (*e.g.*, cash, credit card, debit card), the country to which the funds were transferred, and the manner in which the funds were received (*e.g.*, cash or deposited into a bank account).

This information was then sent to one of the three nationwide credit reporting agencies (NCRAs). The NCRA attempted to match the consumers in the remitter sample with their credit records in the NCRA's files. For those consumers that could be matched, the NCRA merged the complete credit record of the consumer with the RTP data and added a commercially available credit score, the VantageScore (version 2.0). The NCRA then removed any direct identifying personally identifiable information, such as name, address, and Social Security number and created a consumer ID number, solely for this study, that allows all of the remittance and credit history information associated with the same consumer to be identified. The files received by the CFPB contain the remittance histories and credit record information (when available) for each consumer in the remitter sample. None of the files received by CFPB included any direct identifying personally identifiable information about these consumers.

Of the 500,000 people in the remitter sample, only 212,532 (or 43 percent) were matched to a unique credit record. Several factors likely contribute to this low match rate. For example, people who send remittance transfers may be less likely to use the credit sources that trigger the creation of a credit record or some of them may have recently immigrated to the United States and had insufficient time to establish a credit history. Alternatively, the low match rate might reflect incomplete or inaccurate addresses or a lack of other information (such as Social Security numbers) that would have improved the match process. With the data available, it is difficult to determine the extent to which any possible cause is driving this low match rate.

In addition to the credit records of the remitter sample, the NCRA also supplied a sample of 200,000 randomly selected, anonymous credit records (the "control sample"). Like the remitter sample, the control sample includes the entire contents of each credit record, again excluding any directly identifying personally identifiable information, and a VantageScore (version 2.0). Since we cannot determine whether any of the consumers in the control sample sent remittance transfers themselves, this sample does not represent the population of consumers that sent no remittance transfers. However, the control sample can be used to draw comparisons between the credit records of the consumers who sent remittance transfers through the RTP supplying the data and the general population. Because we have data on remitters from only one RTP, the remitter sample does not necessarily represent the population of remitters.

For both the remitter and control samples, credit records were supplied for two points in time, December 2008 and December 2010. We use the later of the two credit record draws to assess each consumer's performance on credit obligations from January 2009 to December 2010 (the "performance period"). Performance over this period can be related to credit record characteristics, including the VantageScore, from December 2008 and remittance transfers made during 2007-2008 to assess the predictiveness of this information.

We assess credit performance during the performance period using the worst performance on any of the consumer's new or existing accounts, which is a commonly used metric in evaluating credit scoring models (Board of Governors of the Federal Reserve System, 2007). "Existing accounts" are those that were open and in good standing at the start of the performance period (December 2008) and "new accounts" are those opened during the first six months of the performance period (January to June 2009).

Each account's performance is classified in one of four ways: "on time," "defaulted," "indeterminate," or "not applicable." Accounts that had at least one payment due during the performance period and where all payments were made as scheduled are classified as "on time." Accounts that were 90 or more days past due or worse during the performance period are classified as "defaulted." Other accounts are classified as "not applicable" if they had no reported payments due during the performance period or as "indeterminate" if they were 30 or 60 days past due, but no worse. This classification scheme – including the classification of accounts that were 90 or more days past due as "defaulted" – is commonly used by industry in building and validating credit scoring models (Board of Governors of the Federal Reserve System, 2007).

Performance for each consumer is similarly classified as on-time, defaulted, indeterminate, or not applicable based on the consumer's worst performing account. Consumers with one or more defaulted accounts are considered to have exhibited "defaulted" performance. Any consumer with at least one on-time account, but no defaulted or indeterminate accounts, is classified as having had "on-time" performance. Otherwise, consumers are considered to have exhibited "indeterminate" or "not applicable" performance depending on whether any of their accounts was classified as indeterminate. Following standard industry practice in building and evaluating credit scoring models, when evaluating the predictiveness of credit record or remittance information, we focus on those consumers whose performance could be classified as on-time or defaulted and exclude consumers with indeterminate or not applicable performance.

Number of Consumers	200,000	500,000
With Credit Records	200,000	212,532
Deemed "Unscorable" by VantageScore	50,892	25,749
Average VantageScore	754	685
Average Number of Accounts	10.4	10.9
Average Age of Oldest Account (Years)	16.5	9.9
Average Age of Newest Account (Years)	4.0	1.6
Average Percentage of Accounts Ever 30+ Days Past Due	31.8	38.6
Percentage of Consumers 30+Days Past Due in the Last 6 Months	20.7	36.6
Percentage of Consumers With a Mortgage	37.0	33.7
Average Number of Credit Cards	3.9	4.2
Average Credit Card Utilization (Balance-to-Credit Ratio)	16.5	26.7
Average Credit Limit on Credit Cards	11,847	8,367
Average Number of Inquiries in Last 2 Years	1.5	3.2

Summary statistics for the control sample and for that portion of the remitter sample that could be matched by the NCRA are provided in Table 1. In comparing these groups it is important to bear in mind that, as previously noted, the remitter sample is derived from one RTP and is not necessarily representative of all remitters. Also, the statistics in Table 1 do not control for income, age, or other characteristics that might help explain some or all of the differences observed between the remitter and control samples.

With those caveats in mind, we note that consumers in the remitter sample with matched credit records have shorter credit histories on average than consumers in the control sample. On average, the oldest account on the credit record of consumers in the remitter sample is about 10 years, 7 years younger than the average age of the oldest account for the control sample. Remitters in our sample also appear to have opened new accounts more recently. The average

age of the most recently opened account is 1.6 years for remitters, compared to 4 years for the control sample.

The credit records of consumers in the remitter sample also tend to have more evidence of past payment delinquencies with respect to the types of obligations reported to NCRAs. On average, the credit records of remitters in our sample indicate that they had been 30 or more days past due or worse at some point on 38.6 percent of their accounts, compared to 31.8 percent for the control sample. Remitters in our sample also are more likely to have been recently delinquent on accounts. Thirty-seven percent of remitters have been at least 30 days past due on one or more accounts in the last six months, compared to 21 percent of the control sample.

Despite these differences, the credit records of consumers in the remitter sample are similar to those of the control sample in several respects (though all the differences in means for the remitter and control samples are statistically significant at the 1 percent level for every variable shown in Table 1). Consumers in the remitter sample have about 0.5 more accounts on average than consumers in the control sample, which indicates that, despite their shorter histories on average, the credit records of remitters whose credit records could be identified are not "thinner" than the control sample. Both groups are about equally likely to have a mortgage (34 percent of remitters and 37 percent of the control sample have mortgages) and have about the same number of credit cards (4 each), though remitters use a larger share of their available credit. Remitters use, on average, 26.7 percent of their credit lines, compared to 16.5 percent for the control sample.

One difference between the consumers in the remitter and control samples is their credit scores. This study uses the VantageScore (version 2.0), which is a credit score produced by VantageScore Solutions, LLC. The VantageScore covers a range from 500 to 990, with higher numbers indicating a lower likelihood of default. Among those consumers with scorable credit records, credit scores for remitters are lower. The average VantageScore for remitters with scorable records is 685, about 69 points below the average VantageScore for consumers with scorable records in the control sample. The lower credit scores for consumers in the remitter sample with scorable credit records suggest that accessing credit will be more difficult for these consumers.

Can remittance histories be used to score otherwise unscorable records?

A group that might benefit from the use of remittance histories in credit scoring models is consumers whose credit records are currently considered unscorable. There is no single definition of what makes a credit record unscorable; indeed, the definition of an "unscorable record" differs across scoring models and any scoring model's exact definition is generally treated as proprietary and not publicly disclosed. Generally speaking, however, credit records with too few accounts or too little recent activity are treated as unscorable by credit scoring models.

There are several reasons why industry model builders might consider credit records like these unscorable. One reason is that the records may provide insufficient information to distinguish consumers who are likely to repay their debts on time from consumers who are more likely to default. If remittance histories can provide sufficient additional information to allow lower-risk consumers to be identified and separated out from higher-risk consumers, then scoring models incorporating both credit and remittance histories might be able to expand the universe of scorable credit records. Such models might increase the willingness of lenders to extend credit to consumers with otherwise unscorable records, thereby increasing access to credit for these consumers.

In this section, we evaluate whether including remittance histories in credit scoring models is likely to increase the predictiveness of the models enough to warrant generating scores for otherwise unscorable credit records. We begin by estimating a credit scoring model that uses only credit history information. This model serves as a baseline for our analysis as it provides an estimate of the level of predictiveness that credit history information alone produces. We then evaluate how large of an increase in predictiveness results when remittance histories are added to the model. If remittance histories substantially increase model predictiveness, then this information may be sufficient to cause model builders to score such otherwise unscorable records.

Our analysis is based on those records in the remitter sample that were matched to the NCRA data but are considered unscorable by the VantageScore model.[1] In the remitter sample, there are 25,749 such records, which constitute about 12 percent of the portion of the remitter sample that could be matched to credit records (and 5% of the total remitter sample). While in principle remittance histories may also have predictive value for consumers who could not be matched to a NCRA file, without such a match (57.5% of the remitter sample), repayment behavior cannot be observed from the NCRA data. Without observing repayment behavior, it is impossible to build or validate models that predict credit performance for these consumers. So, we exclude these observations from our analysis. This limitation in and of itself necessarily limits the usefulness of remittance histories in scoring otherwise unscorable records.

Consumers in the control sample with unscorable credit records are likewise excluded from the analysis but for a different reason. Without the additional information that remittance histories provide, there is little potential to increase model predictiveness for these consumers. Remittance histories only directly affect the credit records of consumers who have sent remittance transfers. Any attempt to expand credit scoring models to incorporate remittance histories would likely focus exclusively on this population.

---

[1] For credit records in our data that do not include a VantageScore, there is a code that indicates why the credit record is considered unscorable. One of the reasons given is that the credit record is for a deceased consumer. We assume that credit records for consumers who appear deceased in 2008 would remain unscorable even if remittance histories are available and consequently we do not include these credit records in our analysis.

FIGURE 1:   AN EXAMPLE OF CALCULATING THE KOLMOGOROV-SMIRNOV (KS) STATISTIC

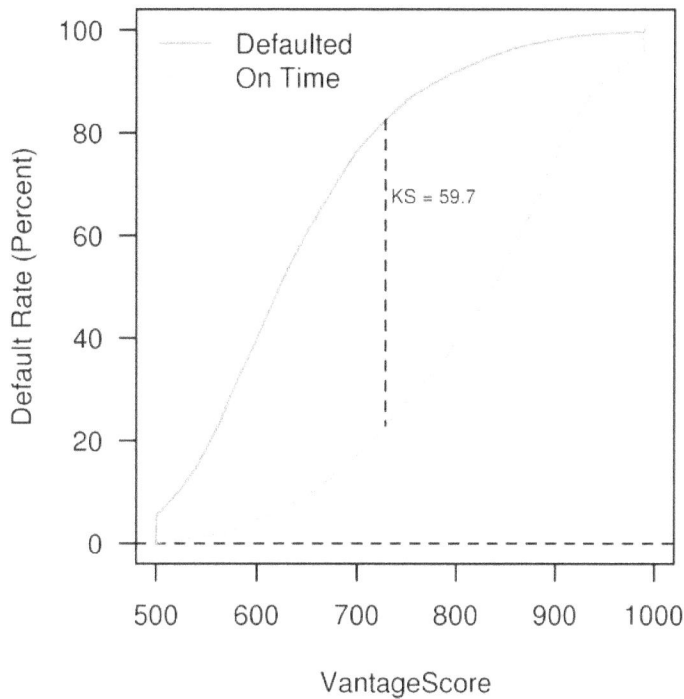

We begin by estimating a "scorecard" specifically for otherwise unscorable credit records in the remitter sample. A "scorecard" is a statistical model that is estimated for a particular segment of scorable credit records. Most credit scoring models are comprised of several scorecards. For example, version 2.0 of the VantageScore, which is used in this study, is made up of 12 different scorecards (VantageScore, 2011). Scorecards allow model builders to vary the credit characteristics used as inputs into the scoring model, and how those characteristics affect the score, with the type of record being scored. For example, credit characteristics related to the amounts and frequency of past delinquencies may be very predictive for people who have had past delinquencies; however, they will have no value in distinguishing good from bad credit risks among records with no past delinquency. For this reason, separate scorecards are generally estimated for credit records with and without past delinquencies. Similarly, if remittance histories were to be used to score otherwise unscorable credit records, it is likely that model builders would develop a separate scorecard that incorporates information about remittance transfers.

To choose the credit characteristics that will be included in the scorecard, we use the model-building methodology developed by the Board of Governors of the Federal Reserve System (2007) to evaluate the effects of credit scoring on the availability and affordability of credit. We use this methodology, the details of which are discussed in Appendix A, to construct a credit scoring model for the portion of the remitter sample with unscorable credit records in 2008. We develop this scorecard using only credit history information to provide a baseline for comparison to measure how much additional predictive power is provided by remittance histories.

The predictive power of the model is assessed using the Kolmogorov-Smirnov (KS) statistic. The KS statistic is defined as the largest difference, across all credit scores, between the cumulative distributions of people with on-time or defaulted performance during the performance period. An example of the calculation of the KS statistic is shown in Figure 1 using the VantageScore and the control sample. The green line shows the cumulative distribution of VantageScores for consumers who defaulted during the performance period; that is, the green line shows, for each level of the VantageScore, the share of consumers who defaulted who had that score or lower. Similarly, the gray line shows the cumulative distribution of scores for consumers who had on-time performance. The largest vertical difference between these lines, which is shown by the vertical dashed line, is the KS statistic. In this example, the KS statistic is equal to 59.7.

KS statistics range between zero and 100 with higher values signifying greater predictive power. At the bottom end, a KS of zero implies that the score distributions are identical for people with on-time and defaulted performance, meaning that the score has no value in terms of separating consumers with on-time and defaulted performance. At the top end of the scale, a KS statistic of 100 implies that the score has achieved perfect separation in that there exists a score below which all of the people with defaulted performance fall and above which are all of the people with on-time performance. Between these two extremes, a higher KS statistic implies that the model does a better job of identifying consumers who are less likely than others to become delinquent.

The scorecard constructed for this study generates a KS statistic of 43.4. Comparing this KS statistic with those generated by other credit scores is complicated by the fact that this statistic was calculated using the same sample of consumers used to estimate the scoring model. Normally, model developers would make use of a "holdout sample," which is a portion of the sample of data that is used to evaluate the fit of the model but that is not used in estimation. Ideally, this holdout sample would include not only a different sample of consumers but would also represent a different time period. KS statistics produced from the sample used to estimate a model are often substantially higher than KS statistics generated from a holdout sample or a sample from a different time period. Unfortunately, the number of consumers in the remitter sample with unscorable credit scores and on-time or defaulted performance is too small to generate both estimation and holdout samples. As a result, this KS statistic likely overstates the predictiveness of this model.

While not a perfect comparison, we can compare the KS statistic produced for this scorecard with the KS statistics produced for the three scorecards that comprise the credit scoring model developed by the Board of Governors of the Federal Reserve System (2007) using the same methodology (the "FRB base model"). Like the scorecard developed here, the FRB base model was developed and evaluated without a holdout sample. The three scorecards of the FRB base model produced KS statistics of 53.5, 61.7, and 72.4.[2] The largest of these KS statistics was produced by the scorecard for credit records with two or fewer tradelines (the "thin" scorecard). Since the population we built our model for is also disproportionately comprised of credit records with two or fewer tradelines, this scorecard is probably the most comparable. But regardless of which scorecard is used for comparison, the credit scoring model developed here produces a KS statistic that is significantly lower. While there is no generally accepted threshold for an acceptable KS, the low KS statistic generated by this model is consistent with the fact that these credit records are considered to be unscorable by the developers of the VantageScore (though there may be other reasons besides a poor model fit that contributed to this decision).

Having established this baseline for the predictive power of a scoring model using only credit histories, we create a new scorecard by adding variables to the model that reflect information about the remittance transfers ("remittance characteristics"). Our analysis focuses on two different remittance characteristics, the number and aggregate dollar amount of remittance transfers sent between January 1, 2007, and December 31, 2008. Since the model including both of these remittance characteristics together produces the higher KS statistic, we focus on the results from that model.

The model with remittance characteristics generates a KS statistic of 43.9, an improvement of 0.5 over the KS statistic from the model built using only credit characteristics. Despite this

---

[2] The three scorecards that comprise the FRB base model include the "thin" scorecard, which scores credit records that have two or fewer tradelines; the "clean" scorecard, which scores credit records that have more than two tradelines without any indication of derogatory activity; and the "dirty" scorecard, which scores credit records with more than two tradelines and indicators of derogatory activity. The thin scorecard generated the highest KS statistic (72.4), followed by the dirty scorecard (61.7) and the clean scorecard (53.5).

improvement, however, the KS statistic for the model with remittance characteristics remains substantially below the KS statistics produced by the scorecards of the FRB base model.

Interestingly, the weights assigned to the attributes for remittance history characteristics are negatively associated with default. This indicates that, among consumers who sent remittance transfers with otherwise unscorable credit records, those who sent more remittance transfers were more likely than those who sent fewer remittance transfers to have had on-time performance on their credit obligations over the performance period. The positive information that remittance transfers convey about this population holds regardless of whether the number of remittance transfers, the dollar amount of remittance transfers, or both are incorporated in the scorecard.

Because there are no hard and fast rules regarding the minimum goodness of fit statistic that would be necessary to make a scorecard commercially viable, we cannot say for certain whether the improvement in the KS statistic is sufficient to cause industry model builders to produce scores for otherwise unscorable consumers who send remittance transfers. However, the fact that the KS statistic generated by the model with remittance transfers remains substantially below any of those generated by the FRB base model suggests that industry model builders are unlikely to view the additional information as sufficiently valuable to warrant scoring the credit records of these consumers.

This analysis comes with important caveats. As mentioned at the beginning of this section, when deciding which credit records will be unscorable (such as, credit records with too few tradelines or no recent account activity), model builders consider more than just the goodness of fit provided by their models. Several other factors may weight against building a scorecard for remitters with otherwise unscorable credit records.

One reason for concern about this model is the small share of consumers with unscorable credit records who had observable performance during the performance period. Of the 25,382 unscorable credit records in the remitter sample, only 6.4 percent (or 1,632 records) had observable performance; that is, they have credit records indicating that they had open accounts during the performance period on which payment performance can be assessed. Since only credit records with observable performance can be used in the model estimation process, the scorecard estimated in this section uses only those 6.4 percent of unscorable records. (In comparison, we observe performance for 72.5 percent of consumers with VantageScores in the remitter sample.)

The consumers who comprise this 6.4 percent are likely not representative of all remitters with unscorable credit records; instead, they are the portion of the unscorable remitter population who were able to obtain credit for at least a portion of the performance period. This may suggest that lenders, who may have access to information beyond what is contained in credit reports (such as, income or employment history), perceived these consumers as being less risky than those who did not have credit over this period.

In such cases, where only a small fraction of a population has observable performance, scorecards may prove unreliable when they are deployed and used to make credit decisions for the entire population (in this case, remitters with otherwise unscorable credit records). For this reason, model builders are generally reluctant to develop scorecards unless performance can be observed for a sufficiently representative portion of the credit records for which the scorecard will apply. This suggests that even if the improvement in the KS statistic is viewed by industry model builders as material, they may still consider this population unscorable.

A second reason for concern about the use of remittance histories in credit scoring models is that incorporating this information may make the model more subject to "gaming." The scorecard developed in this report suggests that, among people with otherwise unscorable credit records, more remittance transfers are correlated with lower levels of default. As a result, if this scorecard were put into use, consumers who send more remittance transfers would receive higher credit scores. A potential consequence of this would be that consumers who desire to artificially inflate their scores may be able to do so by sending money overseas for reasons unrelated to the remitter's desire to assist the recipients of the money or the recipients' need for the money.[3] Done in advance of a credit application, this could allow consumers to obtain credit for which they would not otherwise have qualified. Model builders may be hesitant to use information that allows borrowers to quickly increase their score at relatively low cost.

---

[3] In this respect, artificially increasing the number of remittance transfers to manipulate credit scores would be similar to purchasing authorized user account status on the credit accounts of others, a practice called "piggybacking." In a piggybacking arrangement, the consumer pays a fee to a credit repair company to identify a third party who is willing to add the payer to their account as an authorized user in exchange for a portion of the fee. The payer becomes an authorized user in name only as they receive neither the account number nor an access device (such as a credit card). Nevertheless, by becoming an authorized user, the payer inherits the history of the account on his or her credit report. Done in advance of a credit application, this practice may allow consumers to obtain credit for which they otherwise would not have qualified. Many model builders, including VantageScore and FICO, have sought to revise their models to limit the ability of consumers to use this practice to increase their credit scores. For more information on piggybacking, see Brevoort, Avery, and Canner (2013).

4. Can remittance histories improve the scores of consumers with scorable records?

This section examines the potential for remittance data to improve the credit scores of consumers with already scorable records. Credit scores are empirically derived predictions about a consumer's likelihood of default relative to other consumers; as a result, remittance histories will only affect scores to the extent that the information has value in predicting which consumers will default above and beyond the information already contained in the credit reports used to calculate the score.[4]

In order to boost the credit scores of remitters, remittance histories would have to provide favorable predictive information above and beyond what is already contained in credit records. That is, remitters would have to "outperform" (or experience lower default rates than) other consumers with similar credit profiles. Whether or not this is true can be evaluated by comparing the default rates of consumers in the remitter sample during our performance period to the default rates of consumers in the control sample with identical credit scores.

---

[4] These empirically derived predictions of default apply to the time period used to estimate the model and are not predictions of the level of default in other time periods or other macroeconomic environments. Generally, credit history scores, like the FICO or VantageScores, are best interpreted as numbers that rank order a consumer's likelihood of default relative to other consumers with otherwise similar risk characteristics during the same time period and in similar macroeconomic environments. The actual level of default associated with any score level can and does change over time.

FIGURE 2: CREDIT PERFORMANCE BY VANTAGESCORE FOR REMITTER AND CONTROL SAMPLES

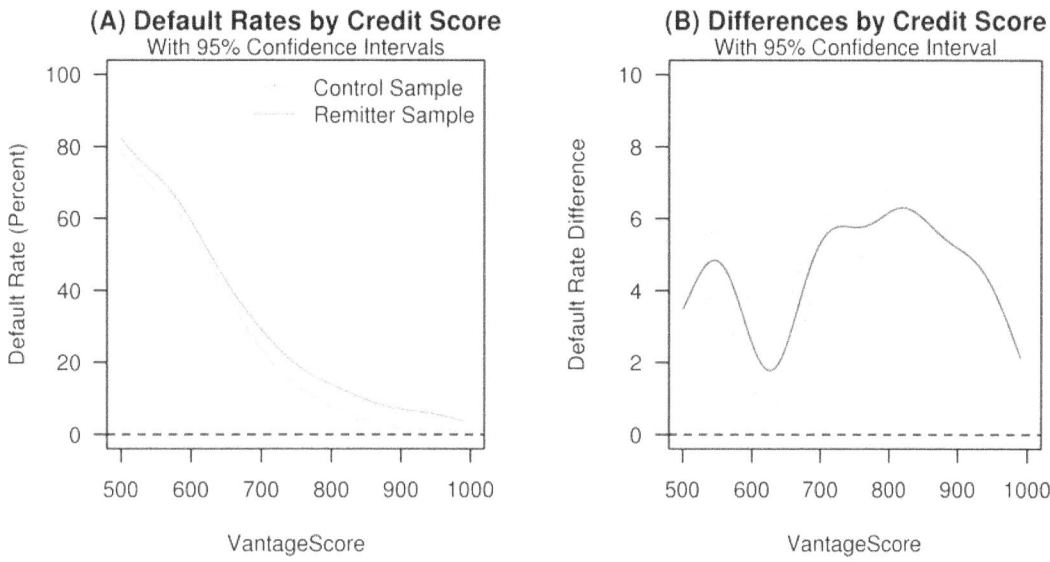

This comparison is shown in Panel (A) of Figure 2. The gray line depicts the relationship between scores and credit performance for the control sample. As the downward slope of the line suggests, consumers with higher VantageScores were less likely to default. For example, almost 24 percent of consumers with a 700 VantageScore defaulted on one or more of their credit obligations during the performance period, compared to 1.8 percent of consumers with a 900 VantageScore. The tendency of default rates to decline as scores increase suggests that the VantageScore rank ordered this population in terms of the default risk these consumers posed.

The green line in that panel shows the relationship between the VantageScore and subsequent performance for consumers in the remitter sample. Like the gray line for the control sample, remitters with higher VantageScores were less likely to default during the performance period. However, default rates are consistently higher for consumers in the remitter sample than they are for consumers in the control sample with identical VantageScores. This is shown in more detail (and in greater magnification) in Panel (B) of Figure 2, which depicts the difference in default rates between the control and remitter samples along with a 95 percent confidence interval. Default rates of remitters with scorable credit records were higher than those of the control sample (indicated by positive values) and those differences are statistically significant.

Information about the remittance transfers themselves, such as how many were sent or the total dollar amounts, could also provide useful information about a consumer's likelihood of default. To assess the value of such information, we use multivariate analyses that can account for differences in remittance activity, as well as control for other factors like demographic characteristics and geography that may be related to default probabilities. We conduct several such analyses, the technical details of which are discussed in Appendix B. The results of these analyses suggest that default rates were 4.7 percentage points higher on average for remitters with scorable credit records than they were for consumers in the control sample with similar credit scores. These higher default rates suggest that adding remittance histories to credit scoring models, like the VantageScore, could *decrease* the credit scores of remitters with scorable credit records.

There are several reasons why sending remittance transfers might be associated with higher default rates. For example, it may be that, rather than providing evidence that someone has excess funds to repay debt, remittance transfers indicate that a larger share of the income of these consumers is committed to other uses. Much in the way a large mortgage payment may make it more difficult for a financially strapped borrower to repay credit card debt (assuming the borrower prioritizes paying his mortgage over his credit card), borrowers who send remittance transfers may have fewer resources to devote to repaying debts. This would be consistent with the positive association in the data between remittance transfers and default among consumers with a scorable credit record.

However, our analysis does not support this hypothesis. If remittance transfers suggest consumers have less disposable income, we might expect to see higher default rates for consumers sending more remittance transfers than for consumers sending fewer. To test this, we estimate models that control for the number or dollar amount of remittance transfers made. The results of these estimations (shown in columns 2 and 3 of Table B1 in Appendix B) suggest that, while generally positive, there is very little relationship between the *amount* of remittance transfers made (expressed either as the number or total dollar amount of remittance transfers) and credit performance.[5]

While consumers with scorable credit records that send many remittance transfers do not appear materially riskier than consumers who send fewer remittance transfers, these results imply that, among consumers with scorable credit records, a consumer who remits even a single

---

[5] The relationship between the dollar amount of remittance transfers and default is not statistically significant. While there is a statistically significant relationship between the number of remittance transfers and default, the coefficient on the number of remittance transfers suggests that this relationship is slight. Each remittance transfer sent increases the likelihood of default by 0.04 percent.

dollar is more likely to default than a consumer who sends no remittance transfers. This suggests that the predictive value provided by remittance histories derives less from the remittance transfers themselves and more from systematic differences in the characteristics of the consumers with scorable credit records who send remittance transfers. That is, remittance histories appear to be picking up a selection effect.

Geography can explain some of this selection effect. The performance period evaluated in this study overlaps the Great Recession, a period characterized by notably higher delinquency rates on mortgages and other types of consumer credit. While the Great Recession affected all areas of the country, delinquency rates were notably higher in some states than in others. In particular, Arizona, California, Florida, and Nevada experienced large house price declines and elevated delinquency rates during this period (Olesiuk and Kalser, 2009). Consumers in the remitter sample disproportionally live in these four states. Almost one-third of the remitter sample with scorable credit records are from these states compared to slightly more than one-in-five of the control sample. Controlling for the state in which the consumer lives reduces the performance difference between the remitter and control samples from 4.7 percent to 4.0 percent.[6] In other words, geography explains some of the performance difference between the remitter and control samples, but most of the difference appears to derive from other factors.

Additional analysis further supports the notion that the negative predictive information conveyed by remittance transfers is the result of a selection effect. Even if one believes that sending remittance transfers signals that a borrower has fewer financial resources to devote to credit obligations, there is little reason to believe that the destination of the remittance transfers should matter. Yet our analysis suggests that where the money is sent matters a lot. For some destination areas we find that remitters with scorable credit records were *less* likely to default than consumers with identical credit scores in the control sample (by 2.6 percentage points). In contrast, for other destination areas we find that remitters with scorable credit records were more likely to default than the control sample (by about 6.2 percentage points in both cases). The fact that the money's destination has predictive value – despite there being no obvious reason why destination should determine credit performance – suggests that these location-

---

[6] Instead of including fixed effects for each state, we estimate a separate VantageScore effect for each state. This approach is more flexible in that it allows different macroeconomic conditions in each state to have different effects by VantageScore. More information about how this was implemented is provided in Appendix A.

related differences reflect selection effects within the remitter sample. These selection effects may reflect differences among the remitter sample in characteristics that are not observable in credit records, such as income, employment, and education. The fact that we do not observe similar relationships between sending remittance transfers and default across remittance destinations suggests that the predictive value of remittance transfers overall has nothing to do with the remittance transfers themselves.

These differences in the observed predictive value of remittance transfers according to where the money is sent also highlight a potential danger in using remittances histories in credit scoring models. The Equal Credit Opportunity Act (ECOA) prohibits discrimination in any aspect of a credit transaction on the basis of race, color, national origin, and other bases. The Fair Housing Act also prohibits discrimination in residential-real-estate-related transactions (*e.g.*, making loans for purchasing, constructing, improving, repairing, or maintaining a dwelling) on the basis of race, color, national origin, or other bases. The use of remittance histories to make credit decisions may have a disproportionate negative impact on certain racial or national origin groups and thereby implicate fair lending concerns. Moreover, a lender's consideration of the geographic destination of an applicant's remittances as part of a credit decision could itself constitute discrimination on the basis of national origin.

In this study, we find differences in the predictive value of remittance transfers among otherwise similar consumers sending remittance transfers to different destination countries. Similarly, in their *Report to Congress on Credit Scoring and Its Effects on the Availability and Affordability of Credit*, the Board of Governors of the Federal Reserve System (2007) found differences in credit performance across racial and ethnic lines, for borrowers with identical credit scores. In both cases, the observed differences may be related to the substantial differences in income, wealth, employment, education, or other characteristics across racial and ethnic groups. They may also (or instead) be driven by differences in the type and terms of credit offered to different racial or ethnic groups. These factors are not reflected in credit records or directly captured by credit scores.

Without demographic information about the people in the remitter and control samples (or sufficient information to construct reliable proxy measures for demographic information), we cannot determine the extent to which (if any) the use of remittance histories in credit scoring models would have a differential effect by race or ethnicity. However, we may be able to roughly approximate the necessary data using the racial and ethnic composition of each consumer's ZIP code using data from the Census Bureau. When these controls for neighborhood racial and ethnic composition are included, we find that they reduce the estimated effect of remittance transfers from 4.0 percent to 3.6 percent. Although the lack of individual-level demographic information renders these results inconclusive, they are consistent with the pattern we would expect to observe if the use of remittance histories in credit scoring models has a disproportionate effect by race or ethnicity.

Other factors also could be contributing to the selection effect that remittance transfers appear to be picking up. One possibility is income, which is not a factor included in credit scoring models. If lower-income borrowers were to exhibit higher delinquency rates than borrowers with identical credit scores and higher incomes, and if remitters tend to have lower incomes than people who do not send remittance transfers, then the predictive value of remittance histories may reflect these income differences. Like race and ethnicity, the credit bureau records do not provide income information. However, we can use neighborhood income from the Census as an approximation. Controlling for neighborhood income, however, appears to have little effect on the estimated relationship between remittance transfers and delinquency.

Regardless of the source of the positive correlation between remittance histories and default for the consumers in our sample (*i.e.*, consumers from one RTP who could be matched to a credit file from one NCRA), the correlation we find suggests that including remittance histories in credit scoring models appears unlikely to improve the credit scores of these consumers.

5. Conclusions

The analyses documented in this report were conducted to further elucidate the issues discussed in the CFPB's *Report on Remittance Transfers* (2011). The results of these analyses suggest that remittance transfers offer little potential to either allow scores to be generated for consumers with unscorable credit records or to improve the scores of consumers with scorable credit records.

The majority of consumers in our remitter sample could not be matched to a credit bureau record. This is because either the remitter did not have a credit record or the NCRA could not uniquely identify the remitter's credit record with the information provided by the RTP. In both cases, there seems little likelihood that remittance histories can enhance the credit scores of these consumers. For remitters without credit records, remittance histories have little potential to produce scores for these consumers, since without credit records to provide credit performance measures model builders cannot construct credit scoring models for this population. For consumers who have credit records, but for whom the NCRA could not match the remittance data, the inability to match credit records with remittance data would preclude using remittance histories in scoring these individuals (though this situation would be mitigated if the use of remittance information in credit scoring incentivized RTPs to collect, and consumers to supply, more or better personally identifying information that made matching feasible).

For the small segment of consumers in our sample with credit records that are considered "unscorable" by the VantageScore credit scoring model, remittance transfers appear to be associated with better credit outcomes. These consumers generally have too few tradelines reflected in their credit records or too little recent account activity for VantageScore to produce credit scores based on credit history alone. Despite the positive information that they provide, however, remittance histories appear to add little to overall model predictiveness, suggesting that industry model builders are unlikely to view the additional information as sufficiently valuable to warrant scoring the credit records of these consumers.

In contrast, for the consumers in our sample who already have credit scores (that is, those consumers whose credit records are considered "scorable" by the VantageScore credit scoring model), the information provided by remittance histories appears to be associated with worse credit outcomes, particularly relative to consumers in the control sample with identical credit scores. This implies that incorporating remittance history information in a credit scoring model would likely lower the credit scores of consumers who send remittance transfers and who have scorable credit records. The lower scores appear to result from selection effects that cannot be explained adequately by the data available but are unrelated to the remittance transfers themselves. Moreover, the data suggest that remittance transfers are likely correlated with race or ethnicity, indicating that the use of remittance histories in credit scoring models might raise concerns under fair lending laws.

The limited value that remittance histories appear to provide for predicting credit performance stands in stark contrast to the potential offered by other forms of alternative data. While concerns have been raised about their use, utility and rental payments have been shown to improve the predictiveness of credit scoring models (Turner, *et al.*, 2006; CFPB, 2011).

A likely reason why these sources of information provide such different value in predicting performance can be found in the nature of the information itself. While rental and other bill payments are not credit *per se*, both fundamentally resemble credit in that they involve obligations to make a series of payments by established due dates. As such, bill payment histories allow the identification of those consumers who missed payments (and if on-time payment information is also reported, it allows consumers who paid on time to be distinguished from consumers who had no payments to make). It seems fairly straightforward to expect that on-time or missed payments for rent or utilities, much like on-time or missed payments for auto loans or credit cards, would convey information about the likelihood that a consumer will repay credit obligations in the future. However, it is important to note that there are unique dynamics around utility payments and payment assistance programs such that full utility credit reporting could harm low-income consumers and undermine the objectives of state utility consumer protections.[7] As discussed in our earlier report (CFPB, 2011), remittance transfers lack this concept of a "missed payment," which makes identifying consumers who are less likely to repay

_____

[7] For additional information about the issues surrounding low-income consumers and full utility credit reporting, see National Consumer Law Center (2009).

debt difficult using these data, as suggested by the low predictive value of remittance histories observed in this study. Future efforts to enhance consumer credit scores by expanding data collections may prove more fruitful if they focus on activities that involve regularly scheduled payments, as opposed to activities involving voluntary payments like remittance transfers.

There are several caveats that go along with this analysis. First, the performance period covered by this study (January 2009 to December 2010) was unusual in that it was a period characterized by abnormally high unemployment and delinquency (particularly on mortgage credit). While we are confident that our results are sufficiently robust to hold in a variety of economic environments, the time period almost certainly had an effect on the magnitudes of the effects that we observe.

Second, the remittance data used in this analysis was taken from a single RTP. Each RTP has its own customer base and these groups of customers may differ substantially in terms of their credit records or likelihood of repaying debt. Likewise, our remitter sample's transaction histories may not represent the complete remittance histories of those remitters, as they may have sent some of their remittance transfers using other RTPs. While we have no reason to believe that our results are dependent upon the choice of RTP, it is possible that data from another RTP, from a representative sample of RTPs, or of consumers' entire remittance histories might yield different results.

Third, our analysis evaluates only the predictive value of remittance histories for two large groups: consumers with and without scorable credit records. Analyses that focus on narrow subsets of these populations might reveal smaller groups for whom remittance histories convey useful, positive predictive information. Evaluating all possible such subgroups is well beyond the scope of this report and the lack of a clear relationship between remittance transfers and reduced delinquency in our aggregate results suggest that any such subgroups would likely be small. Nevertheless, we cannot rule out that there may be some consumers (either with scorable records or without) for whom remittance histories can enhance their credit scores.

Finally, our analysis has only examined the empirical issues with using remittance histories in credit scoring models and has not fully investigated or discussed the potential business and legal issues that would be related to doing so, many of which were discussed in detail in our earlier report (CFPB, 2011). In particular, we have not attempted to ascertain how remittance histories could be used in a credit scoring model in compliance with fair lending laws. If remittance histories are highly correlated with race, color, or national origin, three of the prohibited bases under such laws, using remittance histories could have a disproportionate adverse effect on those bases and might ultimately be found to have an unlawful disparate impact. While some of the questions related to any potential disparate impact are inherently empirical, without additional information about the demographic characteristics of the consumers in the control and remitter samples (or sufficient information to construct reliable proxy measures for such demographic characteristics), we cannot determine whether a disparate impact is likely to result or, if it results, whether the use of remittance histories would nonetheless be permissible under the disparate impact doctrine as "meet[ing] a legitimate business need that cannot reasonably be achieved as well by means that are less disparate in their impact."[8]

---

[8] 12 C.F.R. pt. 1002, Supp. I, § 1002.6, ¶6(a)-2.

6. References cited

Avery, Robert B., Kenneth P. Brevoort, and Glenn Canner (2012) "Does Credit Scoring Produce a Disparate Impact?" *Real Estate Economics* 40(s1): S65-S114.

Board of Governors of the Federal Reserve System (2007) *Report to the Congress on Credit Scoring and Its Effects on the Availability and Affordability of Credit.* Washington, DC: Federal Reserve Board.

Brevoort, Kenneth P., Robert B. Avery, and Glenn Canner (2013) "Credit Where None is Due? Authorized User Account Status and 'Piggybacking Credit,'" *Journal of Consumer Affairs* 47(3):518-547.

Consumer Financial Protection Bureau (2011) *Report on Remittance Transfers*, Washington, DC: Consumer Financial Protection Bureau.

National Consumer Law Center (2009) *Full Utility Credit Reporting: Risks to Low-Income Consumers.* Available at www.nclc.org/images/pdf/credit_reports_full_utility_dec2009.pdf (last accessed 03/04/2014).

Olesiuk, Shayna M. and Kathy R. Kalser (2009) "The Sand States: Anatomy of a Perfect Housing-Market Storm," *FDIC Quarterly* 3(1):30-32.

Turner, Michael A., Alyssa S. Lee, Ann Schnare, Robin Varghese, and Patrick D. Walker (2006) *Give Credit Where Credit is Due: Increasing Access to Affordable Mainstream Credit Using Alternative Data.* Washington, DC: Political and Economic Research Council and The Brookings Institution Urban Markets Initiative.

VantageScore (2011) *VantageScore 2.0: A New Version for a New World of Risk.* Available at www.vantagescore.com/images/resources/VS2.owp_FINAL_4.8.11.pdf (last accessed 12/29/2013).

APPENDIX A:

The model building process

The credit scoring model used in Section 3 of this study was constructed using a methodology developed by the Board of Governors of the Federal Reserve System (2007) and refined by Avery, Brevoort, and Canner (2012). This algorithm was designed to mimic, to the extent possible, the process used by industry model builders in constructing credit history scoring models. While the process actually followed by industry model builders is not as mechanical as that described here, this approach allows us to be transparent about the decisions made in constructing and evaluating the model.

Like the data used by the Federal Reserve Board, the credit records used in this study include a large number of "credit characteristics." Credit characteristics are variables that summarize the contents of each credit record. They are precalculated by the NCRA and supplied to model builders for use in constructing credit scoring models. The credit records provided for this study include 100 such credit characteristics. These credit characteristics include items like the total number of tradelines on the credit record and the total balance on open credit cards.

Each credit characteristic that is included in the model enters the scorecard as a series of "attributes." An attribute reflects a specific range of values, with the attribute assigned a value of 1 if the value of the characteristic falls within the attribute's specified range and zero otherwise. Attributes partition the space of possible values, so that for every credit record a single attribute is assigned a value of 1. All other attributes of that credit characteristic equal zero.

The first step in creating attributes is to determine whether the credit characteristic takes on "non-applicable" values. Non-applicable values arise when the value of a credit characteristic cannot be calculated. For example, if a consumer has not opened an account in the last 6 months, the characteristic "overall balance to credit amount ratio on open trades opened in the last 6 months" cannot be calculated. In these cases, an attribute is created to reflect non-applicable values. For credit characteristics that can always be calculated (such as "total number of trades," which take zero values for consumers with no accounts) attributes for non-applicable values are irrelevant and are not included.

Once an attribute for non-applicable values has been created (if necessary), attributes reflecting (applicable) values of the credit characteristic are created. The attribute creation process begins by creating a single attribute reflecting the full range of possible values of the characteristic. All possible subdivisions of this attribute into two candidate attributes, each covering a compact set of sequential values, are evaluated.[9] This evaluation identifies the subdivision that is the most closely related to future credit performance, as determined by the mean square error. If the difference in mean performance between the two candidate attributes is statistically significant at the 5 percent level then the two candidate attributes replace the single attribute.

The algorithm then evaluates additional possible splits of each attribute (except the attribute for non-applicable values). All possible subdivisions of each attribute are again evaluated, though at this stage only those subdivisions that result in two candidate attributes that maintain monotonicity in mean performance levels across all of the characteristic's attributes are considered. The attribute whose best subdivision reduces the mean squared error the most is replaced by its candidate attributes if the split is statistically significant at the 5 percent level. This process is then repeated until no additional statistically significant and monotonicity-preserving subdivisions are possible.

Once attributes have been created for every credit characteristic, the process of selecting which characteristics will comprise the model begins. When a credit characteristic is selected for the model, all of its attributes are included, except for the attribute reflecting the lowest value of the characteristic which serves as the omitted variable. Following standard model-building practice, we estimate a logit model subject to the constraint that the coefficients across the attributes of each credit characteristic must be monotonic (with the exception of the coefficient on the attribute for non-applicable values).

---

[9] To be considered a candidate attribute, each attribute also had to have at least 5 observations that reflected on-time performance and 5 that reflected defaulted performance. Because of the monotonicity restrictions imposed on the average performance across attributes, this restriction was seldom binding and only then for attribute values at the highest and lowest values for each credit characteristic.

Credit characteristics are added to the model in a forward stepwise manner. We identify which of the 100 credit characteristics (along with an intercept) generates the best goodness of fit. Goodness of fit is assessed in this process using the divergence statistic. Like the KS statistic, the divergence statistic is a measure of a credit scoring model's predictiveness. The credit characteristic that increases the divergence statistic the most is added to the model.

Next, the algorithm evaluates the remaining 99 credit characteristics to identify the one that, along with the credit characteristic that has already been added to the model, produces the largest increase in the divergence statistic. This credit characteristic is then added to the model. Credit characteristics are selected and added to the model in this manner as long as the marginal increase in the divergence statistic that results remains above a threshold of 0.75 percent.

Once this process of adding credit characteristics is complete, each characteristic is again evaluated to ensure that its marginal contribution to the divergence statistic remains above the threshold. This is done by removing each of the n credit characteristics that comprise the scorecard, recalculating the divergence statistic based on a model that includes only the remaining n-1 characteristics, and evaluating whether the implied percentage increase in the divergence statistic from including the characteristic remains above the threshold. Any credit characteristic whose marginal contribution to the divergence statistic is below the threshold is removed from the model. If any credit characteristics are removed, the algorithm then evaluates all of the omitted credit characteristics to assess whether their addition to the model would warrant inclusion.

The process of removing and adding credit characteristics continues until (a) each of the credit characteristics included in the model contributes to the divergence statistic a percentage increase on the margin that exceeds the threshold; and (b) none of the excluded characteristics would improve the divergence statistic by a percentage that exceeds the threshold if included in the model. Once these two conditions are met, the credit characteristics that comprise the model are set.

Once the credit characteristics that comprise the model have been determined, a final version of the logit model is estimated. The coefficients from this estimation are used to generate fitted values (or predictions of the probability of default) for each credit record. These fitted values are used as the credit scores produced by our scorecard.

APPENDIX B:

Multivariate analyses

Several multivariate analyses were conducted to examine the predictive value of remittance transfers for subsequent credit performance for consumers with scorable credit records. In this section, we provide a technical description of the analyses that were conducted and present the results of the statistical estimations that were conducted in more detail.

The multivariate analyses compared the credit performance of consumers in the remitter and control samples who had scorable credit records. Only those consumers with "on-time" or "defaulted" performance during January 2009 to December 2010 are included in these analyses. Consumers with "indeterminate" or "not applicable" performance are excluded. The remaining sample contains 246,968 credit records.

All of the multivariate analyses are conducted using ordinary least squares. These estimations were specified as

$$Delinquency_i = f(VantageScore_i) + X_i\beta + \varepsilon_i \tag{1}$$

where i indexes the consumer. The dependent variable, $Delinquency_i$, is an indicator variable that equals 1 if the consumer exhibited defaulted performance or 0 if on-time performance. Estimated equations include a fixed-effect for each VantageScore level, $f(VantageScore_i)$, so that these analyses are conducted "within score"; that is, we compare differences between the remitter and control samples using consumers with identical scores. The estimations also include a vector of characteristics of interest, X_i, a vector of coefficients that we estimate, β, and a random error term, ε_i.

The first set of analyses is comprised of three specifications that differ in terms of the characteristics that are included in X_i. The first estimation includes only a remitter indicator variable that takes on a value of 1 if consumer i is part of the remitter sample or 0 if part of the control sample. The second estimation includes this remitter indicator and an additional variable equal to the number of remittance transfers the consumer sent during 2007 and 2008. The third estimation includes the remitter indicator and a variable giving the total dollar

TABLE B1: ESTIMATIONS OF CREDIT PERFORMANCE FROM JANUARY 2009 TO DECEMBER 2010

Variables	(1)	(2)	(3)
Remitter Indicator	0.047***	0.044***	0.047***
	(0.002)	(0.002)	(0.002)
Number of Remittance Transfers		0.0004***	
		(8.6e-05)	
Amount of Remittance Transfers ($)			-1.91e-07
			(2.3e-07)
Observations	246,968	246,968	246,968
R-squared	0.302	0.302	0.302

Notes: Standard errors are in parentheses. Statistical significance is indicated by asterisks where *, **, and *** indicate significance at the 10, 5, and 1 percent levels respectively. All estimations include a fixed effect for each level of the VantageScore.

amount of all remittance transfers made in 2007 and 2008. The results of these estimations are presented in Table B1.

Supplementary analyses control for the different macroeconomic environments across states during the performance period. In these estimations, we estimate separate relationships between the VantageScore and performance for each state. Specifically, these estimations are specified as

$$Delinquency_i = f(VantageScore_i, State_i) + X_i\beta + \varepsilon_i \qquad (2)$$

where $State_i$ is the state where consumer i resides and other terms are as described in equation (1). The functional form used for $f(VantageScore_i, State_i)$ allows for a separate fixed effect for each combination of state and VantageScore. These estimations, therefore, implicitly compare the credit performance of consumers in the remitter sample with consumers in the control sample who have the same VantageScore and reside in the same state.

We conduct four estimations using the specification provided in equation (2), each differing in terms of the variables included in X_i. The first estimation includes only the remitter indicator used earlier. The second specification replaces the remitter indicator variable with a series of variables that indicate where consumers in the remitter sample sent their remittance transfers. Since there are too many destinations in the data to present results for them all, indicator variables are included for the five most common regions (Latin America and the Caribbean,

Eastern Asia, South Eastern Asia, Western Africa, and Southern Asia) and for all other destinations.

The third and fourth estimations use data from the 2007-2011 American Community Survey about the characteristics of each consumer's neighborhood. We use each consumer's ZIP code to identify his or her neighborhood and match this to the Census data released for ZIP Code Tabulation Areas. The third estimation includes the remitter indicator variable and variables representing the racial and ethnic composition of each consumer's neighborhood, which enter as a series of variables measuring the share of the neighborhood that is black, Hispanic, American Indian, Asian, Native Hawaiian, other, or multiracial. The fourth estimation includes these same variables and adds a variable representing the median household income in the neighborhood and the total dollar amount of remittance transfers made by the consumer during 2007 and 2008 as a fraction of the median income in the neighborhood. The results of these estimations are provided in Table B2.

TABLE B2: EXPANDED ESTIMATIONS OF CREDIT PERFORMANCE FROM JANUARY 2009 TO DECEMBER 2010

Variables	(1)	(2)	(3)	(4)
Remitter Indicator	0.040***		0.036***	0.036***
	(0.002)		(0.002)	(0.002)
Remittance Destination				
Latin America/Caribbean		0.062***		
		(0.002)		
Eastern Asia		-0.026***		
		(0.004)		
South Eastern Asia		0.028***		
		(0.004)		
Western Africa		0.062***		
		(0.004)		
Southern Asia		-0.002		
		(0.004)		
Other		0.027***		
		(0.003)		
Race or Ethnicity				
Hispanic White			0.044***	0.069***
			(0.005)	(0.005)
Black			0.051***	0.073***
			(0.005)	(0.005)
American Indian			-0.071	0.001
			(0.061)	(0.062)
Asian			-0.072***	-0.084***
			(0.009)	(0.009)
Native Hawaiian			0.292**	0.350**
			(0.148)	(0.148)
Neighborhood Income				5.76e-07***
				(4.43e-08)
Remittance Transfer/ Neighborhood Income				-0.004
				(0.012)
Observations	246,968	246,968	245,074	244,987
R-squared	0.365	0.367	0.366	0.367

Notes: Standard errors are in parentheses. Statistical significance is indicated by asterisks where *, **, and *** indicate significance at the 10, 5, and 1 percent levels respectively. All estimations include a fixed effect for each combination of state and VantageScore. Coefficients for "other race" and "multi race" are omitted to conserve on space.